My Neighborhood
The Police Station

Aaron Carr

www.av2books.com

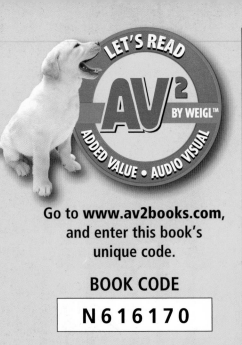

LET'S READ

AV²
BY WEIGL™

ADDED VALUE • AUDIO VISUAL

Go to www.av2books.com, and enter this book's unique code.

BOOK CODE

N616170

AV² by Weigl brings you media enhanced books that support active learning.

AV² provides enriched content that supplements and complements this book. Weigl's AV² books strive to create inspired learning and engage young minds in a total learning experience.

Your AV² Media Enhanced books come alive with...

Audio
Listen to sections of the book read aloud.

Video
Watch informative video clips.

Embedded Weblinks
Gain additional information for research.

Try This!
Complete activities and hands-on experiments.

Key Words
Study vocabulary, and complete a matching word activity.

Quizzes
Test your knowledge.

Slide Show
View images and captions, and prepare a presentation.

... and much, much more!

Published by AV² by Weigl
350 5th Avenue, 59th Floor New York, NY 10118
Website: www.av2books.com   www.weigl.com

Library of Congress Cataloging-in-Publication Data

Carr, Aaron.
 The police station / Aaron Carr.
   pages cm. -- (My neighborhood)
 ISBN 978-1-62127-347-9 (hardcover : alk. paper) -- ISBN 978-1-62127-352-3 (softcover : alk. paper)
 1. Police--Juvenile literature. 2. Police stations--Juvenile literature. I. Title.
 HV7922.C36 2014
 363.2--dc23
                                    2013006708
Printed in the United States of America in North Mankato, Minnesota
1 2 3 4 5 6 7 8 9 0 17 16 15 14 13

032013
WEP300113

Project Coordinator: Megan Cuthbert and Heather Kissock Design: Mandy Christiansen

Weigl acknowledges Getty Images as the primary image supplier for this title. Page 10 Image: pio3 / Shutterstock.com. Page 12 Main Image: justasc / Shutterstock.com.

The Police Station

CONTENTS

This is my neighborhood.

The police station is in my neighborhood.

People call the police station if they are in danger.

They can also go to the police station if they need to talk to a police officer.

I see police officers in my neighborhood.

They make sure people follow the law.

Police officers make sure my neighborhood is safe.

I can spot them easily because they wear a uniform.

Police officers drive special cars.

Police cars have flashing lights and loud sirens.

Some police officers ride bicycles or horses in my neighborhood.

Sometimes people stop and ask the police questions.

If I am lost or hurt I can go to the police for help.

Police help the people in my neighborhood when they do not feel safe.

COURTESY
PROFESSIONALISM
RESPECT

FSD 1566

I can visit the police station with my class from school.

The police officer lets me and my friends sit in a police car.

Police officers take part in neighborhood events.

They visit my school and teach me and my friends about safety.

See what you have learned about police stations and police officers.

Which of these pictures does not show a police station?

KEY WORDS

Research has shown that as much as 65 percent of all written material published in English is made up of 300 words. These 300 words cannot be taught using pictures or learned by sounding them out. They must be recognized by sight. This book contains 44 common sight words to help young readers improve their reading fluency and comprehension. This book also teaches young readers several important content words, such as proper nouns. These words are paired with pictures to aid in learning and improve understanding.

Page	Sight Words First Appearance
4	is, my, this
5	in, the
6	are, call, if, people, they
7	a, also, can, go, need, talk, to
8	I, see
9	make
11	because, them
12	cars
13	and, have, lights
14	or, some
15	sometimes, stop
16	am, for, help
17	do, not, when
18	from, school, with
19	lets, me
20	part, take
21	about

Page	Content Words First Appearance
4	neighborhood
5	police station
6	danger
7	police officer
9	law
11	uniform
13	sirens
14	bicycles, horses
15	questions
18	class
19	friends
20	events
21	safety

Check out www.av2books.com for activities, videos, audio clips, and more!

1 Go to www.av2books.com.

2 Enter book code.  N 6 1 6 1 7 0

3 Fuel your imagination online!

www.av2books.com

24